I0896135

Woodland Wildlife

in filet crochet

Bring the beauty of woodland animals into your home. Simple sewing instructions are given for pillow finishing, or you may choose to frame the designs.

LEISURE ARTS, INC. • Maumelle, Arkansas

What is Filet Crochet?

Filet crochet is a popular form of lace that uses a combination of solid blocks and open spaces to create pictures, motifs and patterns. It's most commonly worked using cotton thread and a steel hook, but is sometimes used for afghans made with yarn. Most often, filet crochet is worked from a square-grid chart which greatly simplifies the instructions to complete a pattern.

How to follow a chart

On filet crochet charts, the blocks are represented by solid squares and the spaces are represented by open squares.

☐ An open square on a chart indicates a space, which is formed by a chain 2 and a double crochet.

■ A solid square on a chart indicates a block, which is formed by 3 double crochets.

Usually you will find a note instructing you to follow the chart from **right** to **left** when working **right** side rows and from **left** to **right** when working **wrong** side rows.

The pattern of blocks and spaces is easily worked by following a graphed chart. The following Basic Chart Stitches list all of the combinations necessary to complete any of the Pillows in this book.

BASIC CHART STITCHES

BEGINNING BLOCK OVER A BLOCK

Ch 3 (**counts as first dc, now and throughout**), turn; dc in next 3 dc.

BLOCK OVER A BLOCK

Dc in next 3 dc.

BLOCK OVER A SPACE

2 Dc in next ch-2 sp, dc in next dc.

SPACE OVER A BLOCK

Ch 2, skip next 2 dc, dc in next dc.

SPACE OVER A SPACE

Ch 2, skip next ch-2 sp, dc in next dc.

Pillow

EASY

Finished Size: Approximately 14" (35.5 cm) square

Shopping List

Thread (Bedspread Weight)

LACE 0

[350 yards (320 meters) per ball]:

- ☐ 1 ball

Crochet Hook

- ☐ Steel, size 7 (1.65 mm) **or** size needed for gauge

Additional Supplies

- ☐ Tapestry needle
- ☐ Sewing needle and matching thread

For Pillow Form:

- ☐ ½ yard (.46 meters) fabric
- ☐ Polyester fiberfill

For Envelope Pillow:

- ☐ ½ yard (.46 meters) contrasting color for pillow front
- ☐ ½ yard (.46 meters) fabric for pillow back

Gauge Information

19 dc and 8 rows = 2" (5 cm)

Gauge Swatch: 2" (5 cm) square

Ch 21.

Row 1: Dc in fourth ch from hook **(3 skipped chs count as first dc)** and in each ch across: 19 dc.

Rows 2-8: Ch 3 **(counts as first dc)**, turn; dc in next dc and in each dc across.

Finish off.

Filet Front

Ch 135.

Row 1 (Right side)**:** Dc in fourth ch from hook **(3 skipped chs count as first dc)** and in each ch across: 133 dc.

Note: Loop a short piece of thread around any stitch to mark Row 1 as **right** side.

Row 2: Ch 3 **(counts as first dc, now and throughout)**, turn; dc in next dc and in each dc across.

Rows 3-56: Follow desired chart, pages 6-14.

Finish off.

Wash and block Filet Front to approximately 14" (35.5 cm) square ***(see Washing and Blocking, page 16)***.

Pillow Form

Using the Filet Front as a pattern, cut 2 pieces of fabric adding a ½" (12 mm) seam allowance on each side.

With **right** sides together, sew around pillow form leaving a 3" (7.5 cm) opening. Clip corners; turn pillow form right side out. Add polyester fiberfill to desired firmness; sew opening closed.

Pillow Finishing

Using the Filet Front as a pattern, cut contrasting color fabric adding a ½" (12 mm) seam allowance on each side.

Using the contrasting color fabric (pillow front) as a pattern, cut fabric for pillow back 6" (15 cm) larger on one side. Matching short ends, fold pillow back in half; cut along fold line. Sew a 1" (2.5 cm) hem along one short edge of both pieces.

Stitch the edges of the Filet Front to the pillow front along the ½" (12 mm) seam allowance.

With the **right** sides together, place back pieces on the front piece so that the two hemmed edges are overlapping in the center of the pillow. Sew around pillow just inside the previous stitching.

Clip corners and turn right side out. Insert pillow form.

Bear

On **right** side rows, follow chart from **right** to **left**;
on **wrong** side rows, follow chart from **left** to **right**.

KEY

- Block (shaded square)
- Space (white square)

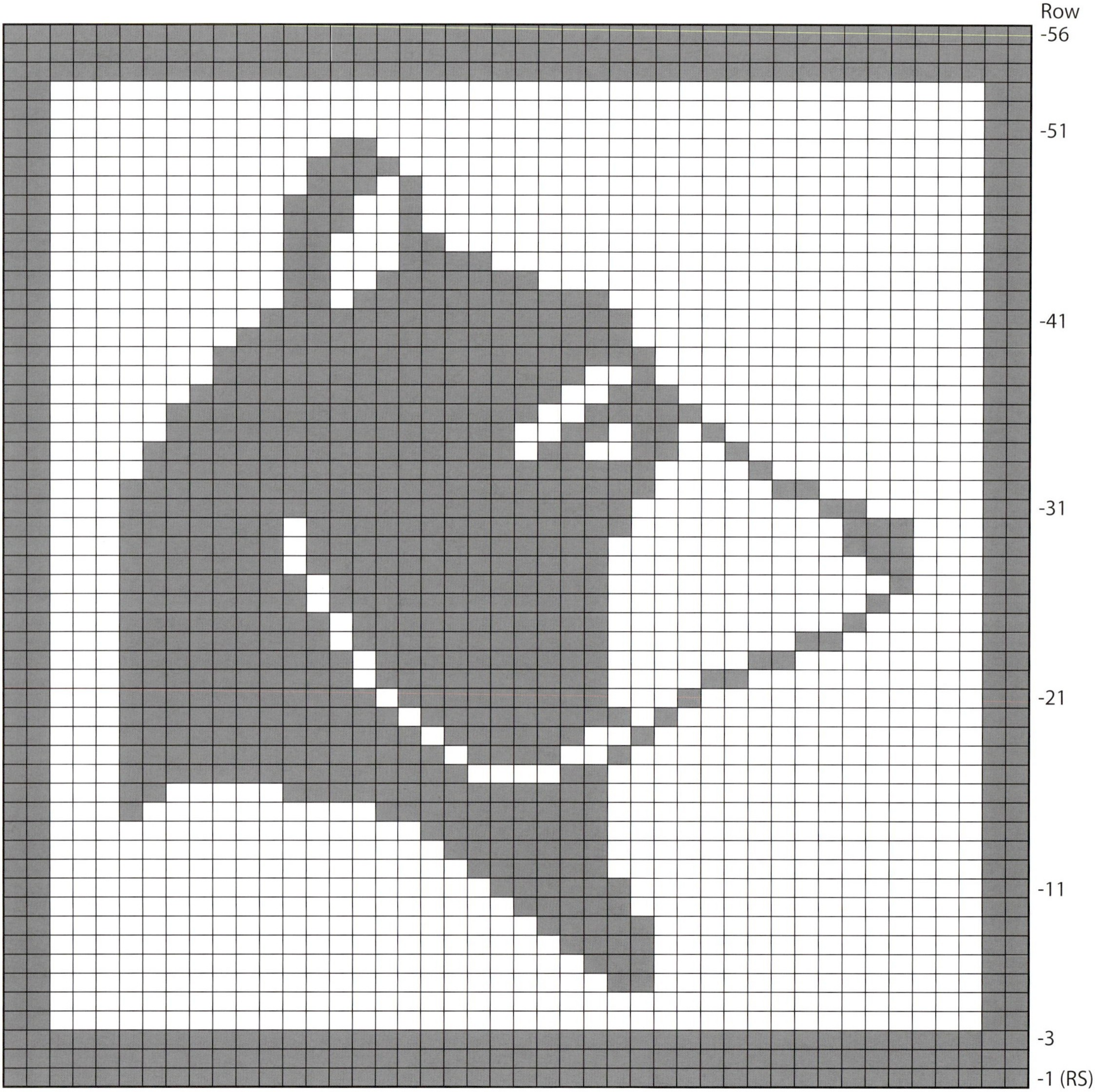

Rabbit

On **right** side rows, follow chart from **right** to **left**;
on **wrong** side rows, follow chart from **left** to **right**.

KEY

- Block
- Space

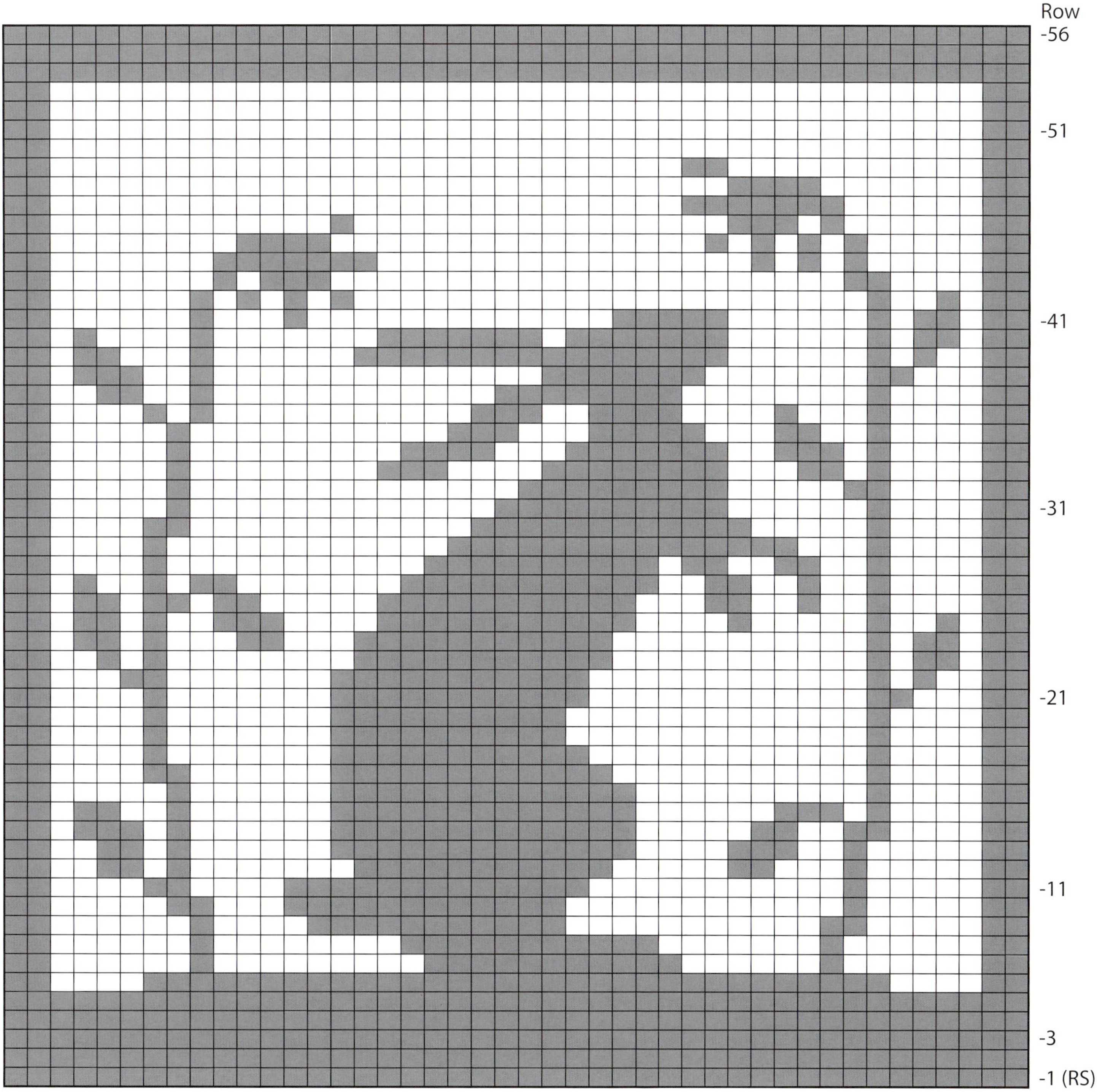

Deer

On **right** side rows, follow chart from **right** to **left**;
on **wrong** side rows, follow chart from **left** to **right**.

KEY

- Block
- Space

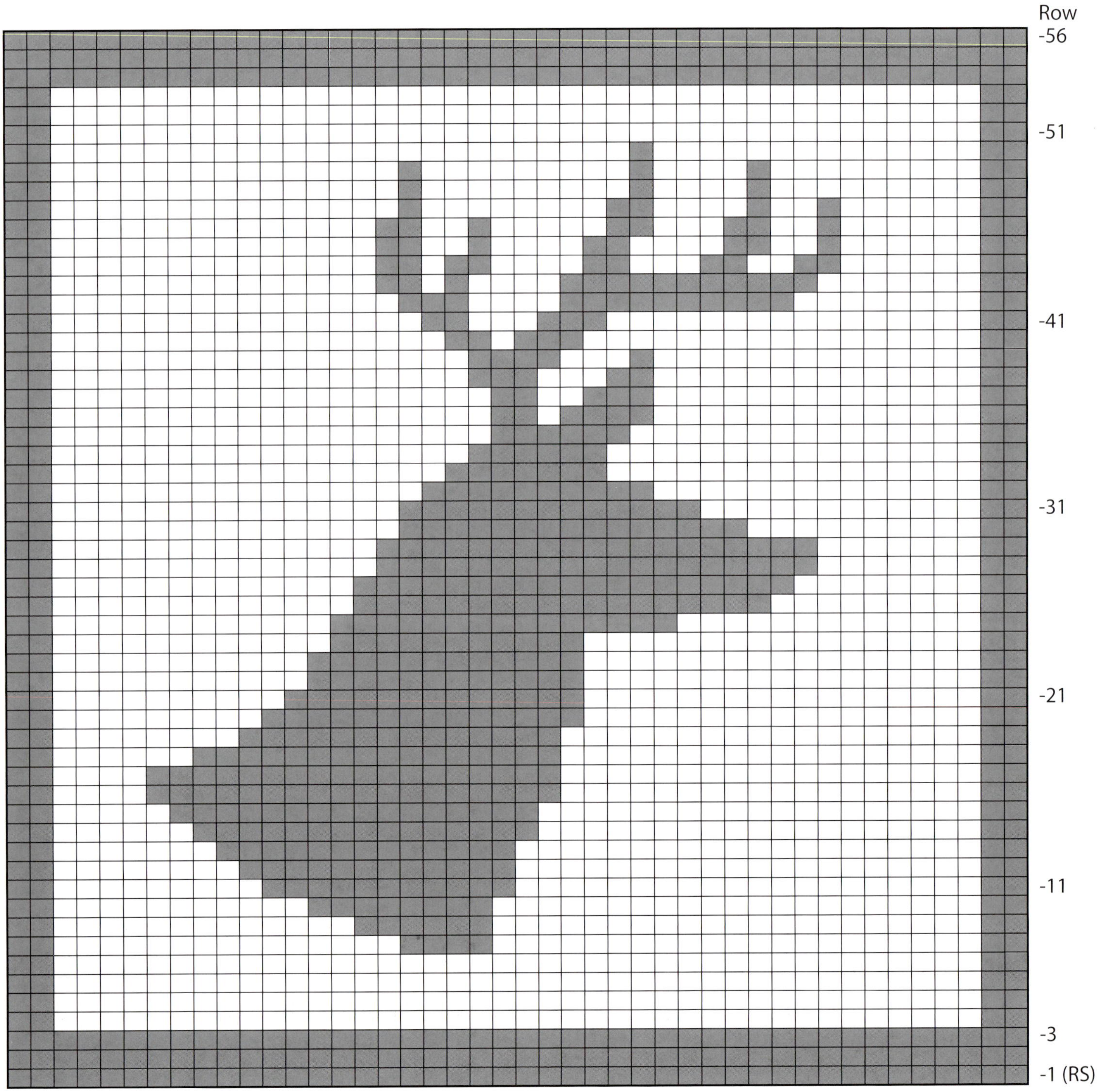

Elk

On **right** side rows, follow chart from **right** to **left**;
on **wrong** side rows, follow chart from **left** to **right**.

KEY

- Block
- Space

Row
-56
-51
-41
-31
-21
-11
-3
-1 (RS)

Fox

On **right** side rows, follow chart from **right** to **left**;
on **wrong** side rows, follow chart from **left** to **right**.

KEY

- Block
- Space

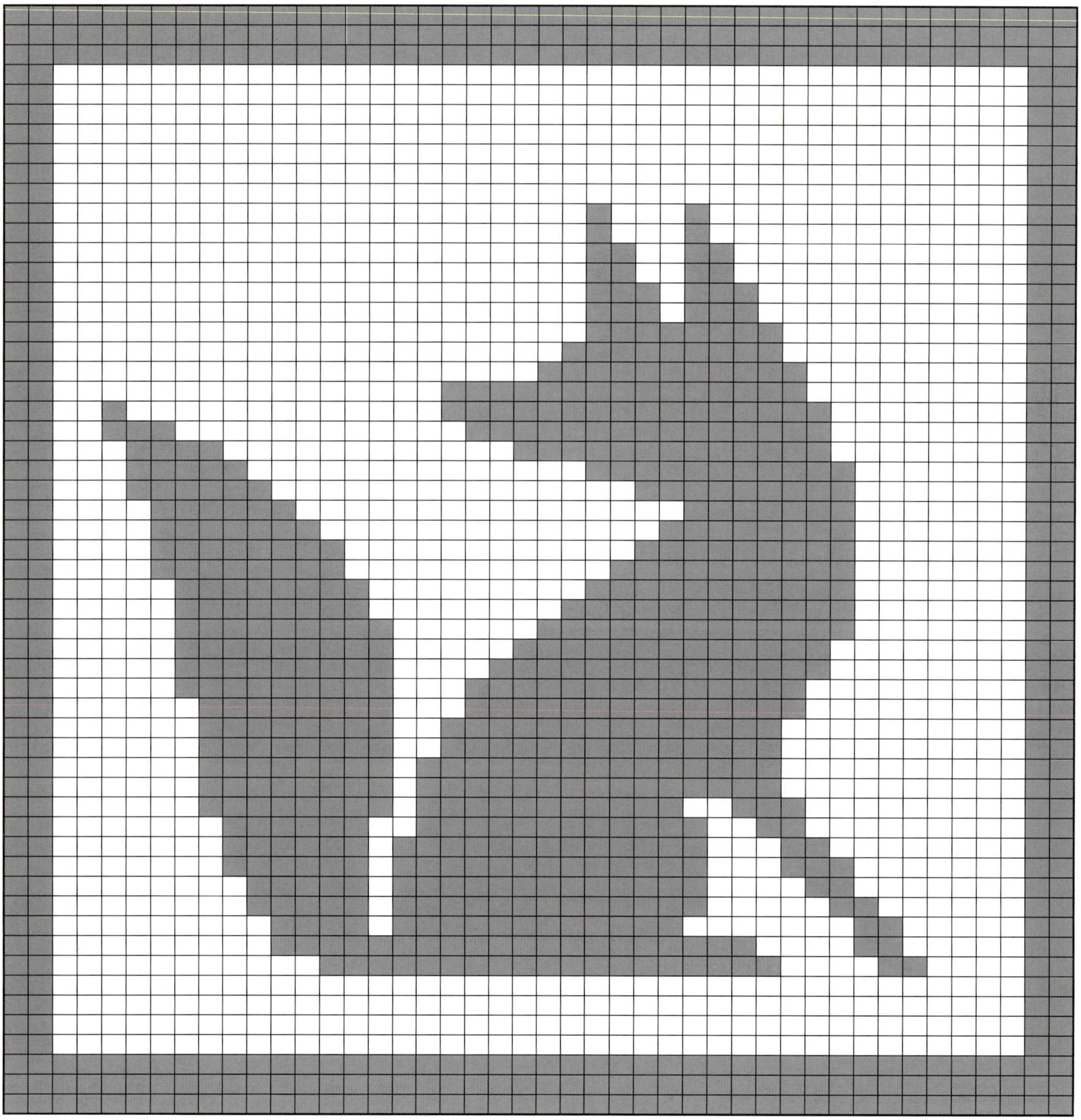

Hummingbird

On **right** side rows, follow chart from **right** to **left**;
on **wrong** side rows, follow chart from **left** to **right**.

KEY

- Block
- Space

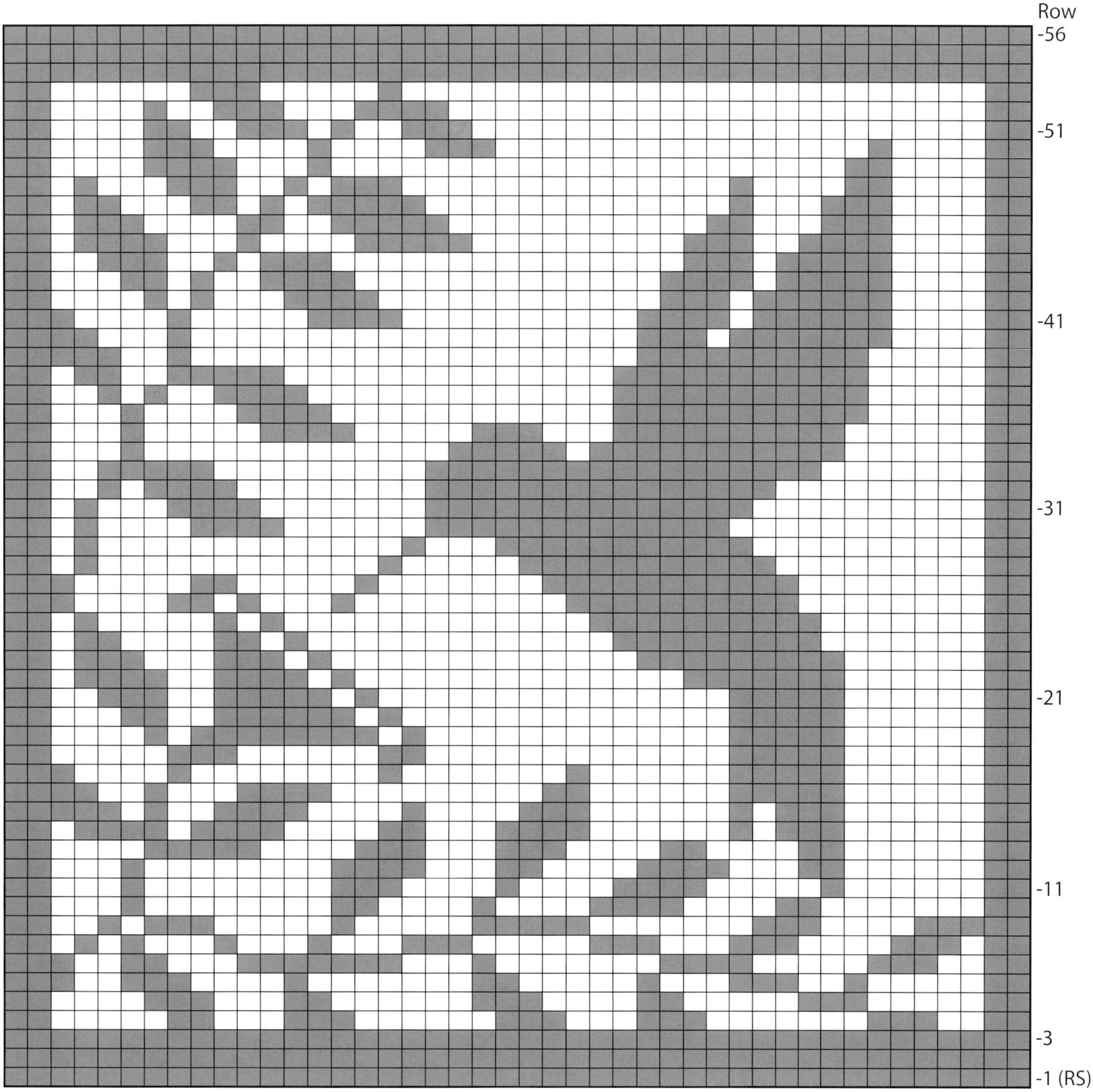

Finches

On **right** side rows, follow chart from **right** to **left**;
on **wrong** side rows, follow chart from **left** to **right**.

KEY

- Block
- Space

Owl

On **right** side rows, follow chart from **right** to **left**;
on **wrong** side rows, follow chart from **left** to **right**.

KEY

- Block
- Space

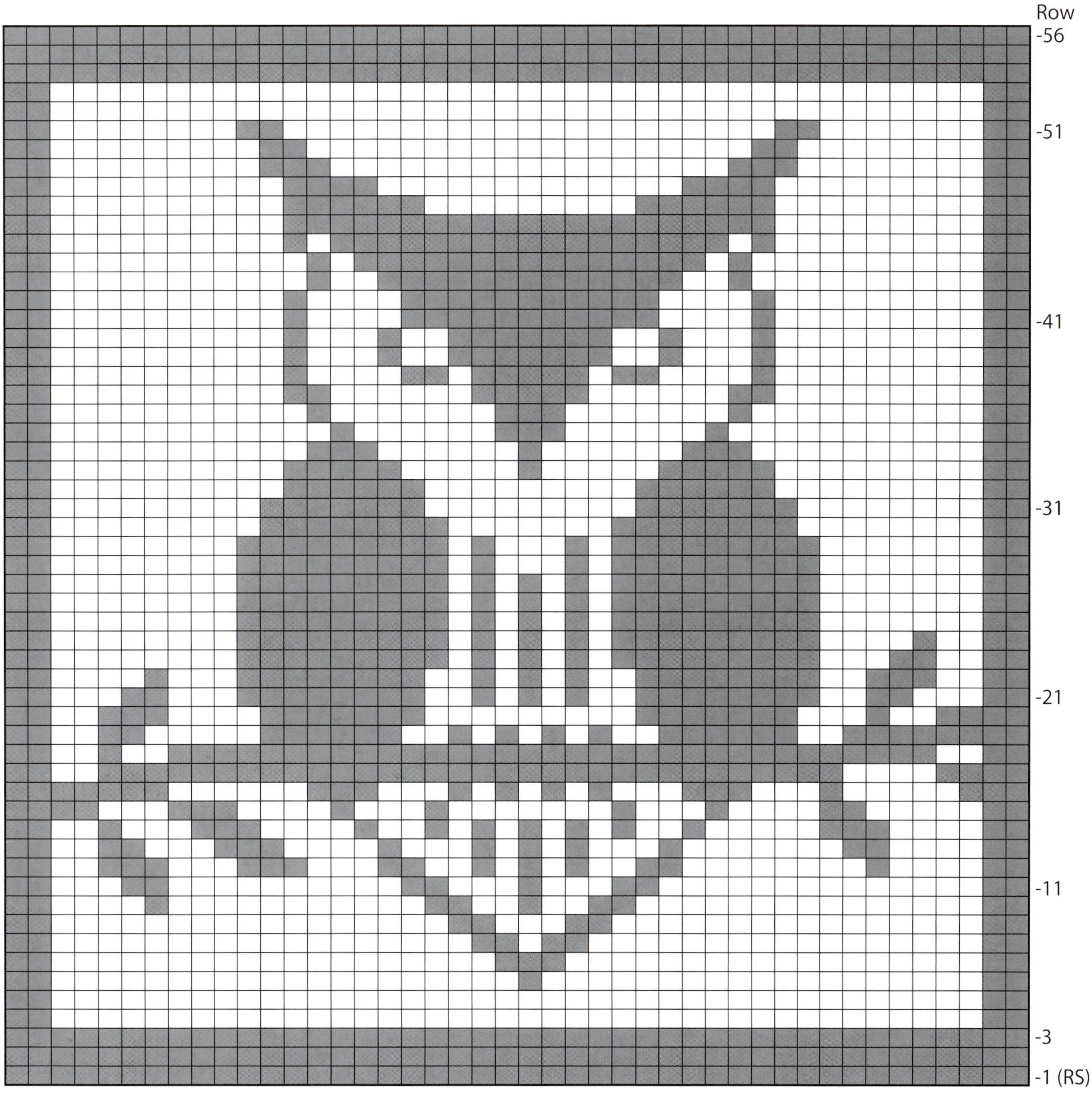

Squirrel

On **right** side rows, follow chart from **right** to **left**;
on **wrong** side rows, follow chart from **left** to **right**.

KEY

- Block
- Space

General Instructions

Abbreviations

ch(s)	chain(s)
cm	centimeters
dc	double crochet(s)
mm	millimeters
RS	Right Side
sp(s)	space(s)

Symbols & Terms

( ) or **[ ]** — contains explanatory remarks.

colon (:) — the number(s) given after a colon at the end of a row denote(s) the number of stitches you should have on that row.

CROCHET TERMINOLOGY		
UNITED STATES		INTERNATIONAL
slip stitch (slip st)	=	single crochet (sc)
single crochet (sc)	=	double crochet (dc)
half double crochet (hdc)	=	half treble crochet (htr)
double crochet (dc)	=	treble crochet (tr)
treble crochet (tr)	=	double treble crochet (dtr)
double treble crochet (dtr)	=	triple treble crochet (ttr)
triple treble crochet (tr tr)	=	quadruple treble crochet (qtr)
skip	=	miss

Gauge

Exact gauge is **essential** for proper size. Before beginning your project, make the sample swatch given in the individual instructions in the thread and hook specified. After completing the swatch, measure it, counting your stitches and rows carefully. If your swatch is larger or smaller than specified, **make another, changing hook size to get the correct gauge**. Keep trying until you find the size hook that will give you the specified gauge.

Yarn Weight Symbol & Names	LACE 0	SUPER FINE 1	FINE 2	LIGHT 3	MEDIUM 4	BULKY 5	SUPER BULKY 6	JUMBO 7
Type of Yarns in Category	Fingering, size 10 crochet thread	Sock, Fingering, Baby	Sport, Baby	DK, Light Worsted	Worsted, Afghan, Aran	Chunky, Craft, Rug	Super Bulky, Roving	Jumbo, Roving
Crochet Gauge* Ranges in Single Crochet to 4" (10 cm)	32-42 sts**	21-32 sts	16-20 sts	12-17 sts	11-14 sts	8-11 sts	6-9 sts	5 sts and fewer
Advised Hook Size Range	Steel*** 6 to 8, Regular hook B-1	B-1 to E-4	E-4 to 7	7 to I-9	I-9 to K-10½	K-10½ to M/N-13	M/N-13 to Q	Q and larger

*GUIDELINES ONLY: The chart above reflects the most commonly used gauges and hook sizes for specific yarn categories.

** Lace weight yarns are usually crocheted with larger hooks to create lacy openwork patterns. Accordingly, a gauge range is difficult to determine. Always follow the gauge stated in your pattern.

*** Steel crochet hooks are sized differently from regular hooks–the higher the number, the smaller the hook, which is the reverse of regular hook sizing.

STEEL CROCHET HOOKS																
U.S.	00	0	1	2	3	4	5	6	7	8	9	10	11	12	13	14
Metric - mm	3.5	3.25	2.75	2.25	2.1	2	1.9	1.8	1.65	1.5	1.4	1.3	1.1	1	.85	.75

BEGINNER	Projects for first-time crocheters using basic stitches. Minimal shaping.
EASY	Projects using yarn with basic stitches, repetitive stitch patterns, simple color changes, and simple shaping and finishing.
INTERMEDIATE	Projects using a variety of techniques, such as basic lace patterns or color patterns, mid-level shaping and finishing.
EXPERIENCED	Projects with intricate stitch patterns, techniques and dimension, such as non-repeating patterns, multi-color techniques, fine threads, small hooks, detailed shaping and refined finishing.

FILET CROCHET TIP

To help achieve straight edges, turn your work counterclockwise at the end of each row and work the last stitch in the back loop and back bar of the last dc (third chain of turning ch-3).

WASHING

Despite the fragile appearance of threadwork, it is very durable and can last a lifetime with proper care. Always wash the item when you finish crocheting it. The thread undergoes a lot of handling during construction, and the oils from your hands can soil the work. Washing and blocking helps to "set" the stitches, resulting in a neat and uniform appearance and giving your work a "professional" look.
Using a mild detergent and warm water (never hot!), gently squeeze suds through the piece. Being careful not to rub, twist or wring, rinse the piece several times in cool, clear water. Roll it in an absorbent towel and gently press out the excess moisture.

BLOCKING

After washing the design and while it is still wet, place it on a blocking board, an ironing board, or a piece of cardboard covered with a towel. Pin the design to the size indicated in the individual instructions with rustproof pins. Make sure that all of the stitches and rows in the design are straight. Allow the design to dry completely.

Thread Information

Each Pillow Front in this book was made using Aunt Lydia's® Classic Crochet Cotton Thread™, size 10 (color #12 Black). Any brand of bedspread weight cotton thread may be used. It is best to refer to the yardage/meters when determining how many balls to purchase. Remember, to arrive at the finished size, it is the GAUGE/TENSION that is important, not the brand of thread.

Meet Lisa Meadows

Lisa Meadows has been enjoying crochet and other crafts for as long as she can remember. "I was raised by my grandmother, who was an amazing woman who had a love of crafting and sharing her talents with others," she said.

"I enjoy cross stitching, tatting, painting, sewing, paper crafts, and in general, just about anything that I can attempt to create something new." Lisa says her designing is driven by "the challenge of taking a wisp of an idea, studying and learning how to manipulate a textile of some sort to come out with an end project. And then, taking that learned process and evolving it to even something else."

Her filet crochet animal designs (except for the bear) were inspired by creatures she has viewed from the back porch of her country home in Kentucky, where she and a partner run an upholstery shop.

Her advice to everyone is this: "CREATE — even if it is something small, it can feel grand."

We have made every effort to ensure that these instructions are accurate and complete. We cannot, however, be responsible for human error, typographical mistakes, or variations in individual work.

Production Team: Technical Editor/Writer - Linda A. Daley; Editorial Writer - Susan Frantz Wiles; Senior Graphic Artist - Lora Puls; Photo Stylist - Lori Wenger; and Photographer - Jason Masters.

Copyright © 2016 by Leisure Arts, Inc., 104 Champs Blvd., STE 100, Maumelle, AR 72113-6738, www.leisurearts.com. All rights reserved. This publication is protected under federal copyright laws. Reproduction or distribution of this publication or any other Leisure Arts publication, including publications which are out of print, is prohibited unless specifically authorized. This includes, but is not limited to, any form of reproduction or distribution on or through the Internet, including posting, scanning, or e-mail transmission.